CABLE CARS—Synonymous with the image of San Francisco is the ageless attraction of its cable car rail system. This unique transit system is used regularly by residents and is a fascinating experience for visitors.

MARKET STREET &
POWELL
AND
MARKET 13
HYDE AND BEACH
FISHERMANS
WHARF
Schweppes
FISHERMANS WHARF

GOLDEN GATE BRIDGE—This magnificent structure, created against enormous odds, is one of America's famous landmarks. The bridge is etched in the memories of America's returning military and civilian personnel as their welcome-home symbol following duty in the Pacific theater. This engineering marvel, open to pedestrians and cyclists, is used by more than 100,000 cars each day.

SAN FRANCISCO OAKLAND BAY BRIDGE

This dramatic double-decked bridge is 8½ miles long in total. It is the major link between two of America's finest cities.

SAN FRANCISCO BAY

San Franciscans are blessed with having this lovely bay at their doorstep. In addition to serving the commercial needs of worldwide shipping, cruise ships, intra-bay ferries and tour boats, it affords pleasure-boaters an outlet for their participation. Colorful sails dot the bay in harmony with ships from far off foreign ports.

Entrance to main prison cell

Broadway cell block

"D" block-Solitary confinement

A typical cell

Path to laundry and factory

ALCATRAZ—This world-famous island, in San Francisco Bay, was known as "The Rock". In its days as a federal prison it imprisoned many of America's most notorious criminals. Because of the treacherous waters between it and the mainland, escape was considered impossible. The island is now administered by the National Park Service and guided tours are offered.

View of City through bars

PIER 39—This pedestrian pier, themed to a turn-of-the-century waterfront thoroughfare, is a tourist delight. Countless shops and restaurants, together with a large marina, combine to create a delightful milieu for hours of pleasure.

FISHERMAN'S WHARF—This bustling area is a mecca of interests for the tourist and resident alike. Museums, a fishing fleet, gourmet restaurants, street vendors with steaming vats of fresh seafood delicacies, nearby Pier 39 and Ghirardelli Square offer a charming and fulfilling excursion.

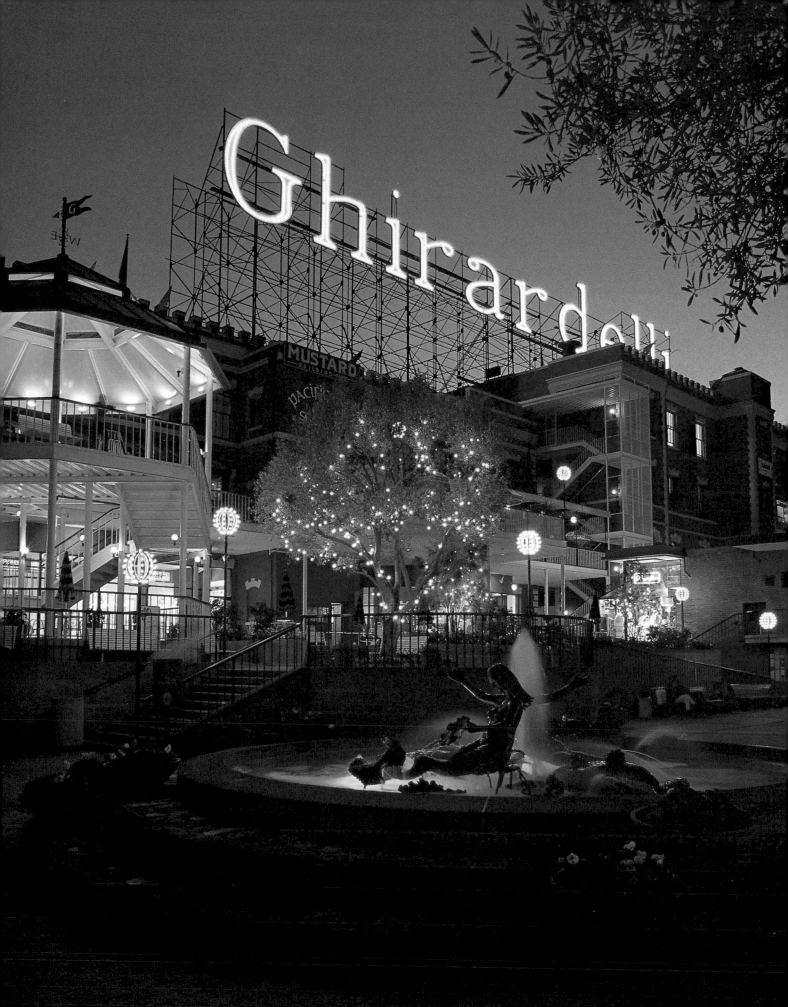

GHIRARDELLI SQUARE—This colorful complex, a former chocolate factory and woolen mill, has been beautifully restored and is home to outstanding restaurants, shops and services. The Cannery, an adjacent former canning factory, is of like restoration and interest.

LOMBARD STREET— This world famous brick lined street between Hyde and Leavenworth makes eight switchback turns in one block. These photographs capture the magnificent hydrangeas in full bloom. Pictured above is St. Peter and Paul Church located in nearby Washington Square Park.

COIT TOWER

Standing tall atop Telegraph Hill, this landmark tower is named for an early pioneer, Lillie Hitchcock Coit. As a little girl she was rescued from a hotel fire and became the self appointed mascot of San Francisco's fire department. She died an elderly woman, honored by the department she loved.

VICTORIAN HOMES—

Commencing in the middle-1800's, more than 40,000 Victorian-style homes were built in San Francisco. Many exist today; colorful, distinct and beautifully preserved by their owners. They speak to one facet of the unique heritage of this lovely city.

MISSION DOLORES— Founded as Mission San Francisco de Asis in 1776, the old mission is the oldest building still standing in the city. Located next door is the beautiful Basilica that was rebuilt after the 1906 earthquake. A unique cemetery garden is located behind the old mission.

ST. MARY'S CATHEDRAL—Soaring up to the height of 200 feet and covering two city blocks 440 feet wide, the dramatic design of St. Mary's Cathedral is truly an architectural wonder of great beauty. The present Cathedral is four times the size of the Old St. Mary's destroyed by fire on September 7, 1962.

THE CABLE CAR BARN AND MUSEUM— Located at Washington and Mason Streets, this brick building is the home to San Francisco's famous cable cars and the interesting museum full of historical information and displays. Also located here is the machinery that runs the entire cable car system.

THE CONSERVATORY OF FLOWERS— Located in Golden Gate Park, this magnificent Victorian style glass structure is home to thousands of species of tropical plants and seasonal flowers. The various plantings of flowers in the beds in front of the conservatory are spectacular in every season.

GOLDEN GATE PARK—This magnificent park of more than 1,000 acres is one of the nation's premier park areas. The Flower Conservatory, Japanese Tea Garden, de Young Memorial Museum, California Academy of Sciences and Strybing Arboretum and Botanical Gardens, are placed in a setting of lakes, trees, floral plantings and activity areas.

CLIFF HOUSE — This restaurant, lounge and gift shop is a popular tourist stop. Located on Point Lobos, it overlooks the blue Pacific and the famous Seal Rocks, with their outspoken populace of Sea Lions.

San Francisco is famous for its neighborhoods and shopping streets. Pictured top left is Union Street with its smart shops and trendy restaurants and bars. Pictured top right and below is "The Castro", the centerpiece of the city's gay population.

THE CITY BEAUTIFUL—Whether viewed from a helicopter or high on Twin Peaks, the "City by the Bay" is a breathtaking sight. The hills, sparkling homes, dynamic architecture and assemblage of instantly recognizable landmarks create a panorama of lasting memory.

ONE WAY

CATHAY HOUSE
RESTAURANT · COCKTAILS

CHINATOWN—The largest Chinese community outside of Asia is here, in San Francisco. Here is the exotic glamour of the Far East with its customs, architecture, essences, foods, skills, and products. Residents and visitors enjoy excellent cuisine and shopping adventures.

SAN FRANCISCO BAY AREA EARTHQUAKE OCTOBER 17, 1989—

The earth shook at exactly 5:04 p.m. on October 17, 1989 just before the start of the third game of the World Series between the Giants and the A's. The earthquake measured 7.1 on the Richter scale. While 95% of the City escaped serious damage, the Marina District, on landfill, suffered the most destruction. Also shown are the collapsed 880 Freeway and the 50-foot section of the Bay Bridge that collapsed. The bridge was repaired in record time, and reopened one month later.

EXAMINER BAY TO BREAKERS

Held every year in May, this 7.5 mile run begins at the Bay in the Financial District and crosses the City through Golden Gate Park ending at the ocean. Over 75,000 runners of various shapes, sizes and abilities participate, making this the largest footrace of its kind in the world.

STREET ARTISTS—Probably nowhere else can one encounter the inventive, amusing and entertaining artists on the streets of the city.

PALACE OF LEGION OF HONOR—The permanent exhibit of French art and antiques is rivaled by the magnificence of the structure itself.

LOUISE M. DAVIES SYMPHONY HALL—This famous building, which seats 3,000 persons, is the home of the San Francisco Symphony.

CITY HALL—This imposing structure, built of granite in the French Renaissance style, is the seat of city government.

WAR MEMORIAL OPERA HOUSE—The home of the San Francisco Opera was selected as the site for the signing of the United Nations Charter in 1945.